MARY MOUSER

A Star in the Making

Patricia C. Soo

COPYRIGHT

All rights reserved. No part of this book may be reproduced, distributed, or transmitted in any form or by any means, including photocopying, recording, or other electronic or mechanical methods, without the prior written permission of the author, except in the case of brief quotations used in reviews or articles. This book is a work of biographical storytelling and is not an official autobiography. The content is based on publicly available information, research, and creative interpretation. Any resemblance to actual conversations, thoughts, or private moments is purely coincidental.

DISCLAIMER

This book, MARY MOUSER: A Star in the Making, is a work of biographical storytelling written in a first-person narrative style. It is not an official autobiography and has not been directly authored or endorsed by any individual associated with the subject. The content is based on publicly available information, research, and creative interpretation to provide an engaging and immersive reading experience.

While every effort has been made to ensure accuracy regarding events, timelines, and details, some elements have been adapted or reconstructed for narrative purposes. Any opinions, reflections, or emotions expressed in this book are fictionalized representations crafted for storytelling.

This book is intended for informational and entertainment purposes only and does not claim to reflect the personal views, thoughts, or exact words of the individuals featured. The author and publisher disclaim any responsibility for misinterpretation or assumption that this book constitutes an official personal account.

All trademarks and names used in this book are the property of their respective owners and are used solely for descriptive and informational purposes. No endorsement or affiliation with any individual, organization, or entity is implied.

Table Of Contents

Introduction

Chapter 1

Chapter 2

Chapter 3

Chapter 4

Chapter 5

Chapter 6

Chapter 7

Chapter 8

Conclusion

Introduction

"Every great dream begins with a dreamer."

I've always thought that dreams have great power. The kind of dreams that inspire us to rise in the morning, persevere through difficult times, and have faith in something greater than ourselves—not just the ones that occur to us while we're asleep. When I reflect on my journey, I see that every accomplishment I've made, from landing my first movie role to joining a global phenomenon, started with a straightforward but impactful dream.

I grew up in a small American town and never could have predicted the course of my life. I didn't have a clear route to stardom or the luxury of a large Hollywood family. I did, however, have a strong love for telling stories, a strong desire to perform, and the encouragement of a family that had faith in me even when I didn't. In retrospect, it's nearly impossible to identify the apprehensive and nervous girl who first entered the world of acting. With a camera in front of me and lofty aspirations, I was a young child hoping to succeed.

The difficulties, discoveries, and turning points in that journey are all reflected in this book. It's about the work, the heartache, the tenacity, and the small victories that add up to something greater than we could have ever imagined; it's not just about the glamour and glitz of Hollywood. My story is one of gradual ascent rather than quick success, where each setback served as a teaching moment and each victory, no matter how minor, indicated that I was headed in the right direction.

I had no idea if I would ever make it when I first started trying out. If anyone would notice what I had to offer, I didn't know. I recall sitting in the waiting areas with other children who appeared to be much more self-assured and prepared. However, I had a glimmer of hope that I could prove myself if I were given the opportunity. It took years, actually, but with each callback, rejection, and audition, I began to learn what it meant to stand up for what I wanted.

The day I learned I had been cast in Cobra Kai is still fresh in my mind. It was a moment that seemed to be the culmination of everything. I was going to be a part of a project that would forever alter my life after all the auditions, hardships, highs, and lows. I didn't anticipate, however, how much Samantha LaRusso would test me as a person as well as an actress. The actual show grew into something greater than we could have ever imagined. It developed into a cultural movement rather than merely another old film revival. I was also given the chance to develop a character in a way I had never done before during that time.

Samantha wasn't your average hero. She wasn't flawless. She was imperfect; she battled with her identity, family, friendships, and the traditions of those around her. What made her so real to me was her humanity and complexity. I also became aware that I was developing both on and off screen as I started to comprehend her. Her struggles were similar to many of mine, and depicting her made it clearer to me how important it is to accept flaws and learn from them. I could really identify with her because she was a young woman attempting to figure out who she was in the world, not a superhero.

Even though Cobra Kai gave me opportunities, that wasn't the whole story. I was able to experiment with more than just the roles I played thanks to acting. It provided me with a voice and a chance to express my ideas to the world. It made it possible for me to interact with people in ways I never would have thought possible. During that journey, social media emerged as a surprising yet crucial tool. I had the opportunity to speak with fans face-to-face, share my experiences, and learn about their stories. The love and support of my followers kept me going even though it wasn't always easy—there were moments when the pressure of being in the spotlight felt unbearable. I soon came to understand that my story was no longer unique to me; it was shared with a large number of people who had been influenced by the roles I played and the values I upheld.

"The road to success is always under construction," goes a famous quote. For me, that couldn't be more accurate. There isn't a foolproof recipe for success in Hollywood. There isn't a recipe for success. The difference frequently boils down to perseverance, timing, and an unwavering belief in oneself. For every actor who "makes it," there are hundreds who don't. It all boils down to being receptive to learning and development, though. This journey has no destination. Though I'm aware that I'm only beginning, the experiences, people, and lessons I've encountered have all molded me into the person I am today.

This book is a look to the future as much as a reflection of my past. I hope that by sharing my story, others will realize that anything is achievable if you're willing to put in the necessary effort. I'm still dreaming and working toward more. There are many obstacles in the way, and it's not always simple. What matters most, though, is the path you take to reach your destination.

Let's get started. Allow me to walk you through my life's journey, including the lessons I've learned, the victories I've celebrated, and the dreams I still have. Because I want you to realize that there is always space for improvement and an opportunity to realize your dreams, regardless of where you are in your own journey.

Come on.

Chapter 1

Beginnings in the Spotlight

"The moment you stop dreaming is the moment you stop growing."

I can still remember the first time I had a real dream—one that wasn't just a fleeting thought or a daydream. I was about six years old, sitting cross-legged on the floor of my bedroom, watching TV when I first saw someone on screen that felt larger than life. It wasn't just the characters they were playing, it was the way they made you feel—like anything was possible. It hit me then, deep in my gut: I wanted to do that. I wanted to make people feel what I was feeling right then. I wanted to be an actress.

As a child, everything seemed like an adventure, and yet I had no idea that this one dream would lead me down a path so unexpected and transformative. Growing up in the suburbs, acting was as far from my daily life as you could get. My world was small, centered around my family, school, and weekends spent running around with neighborhood friends. But somewhere in the back of my mind, I always knew there was something more out there. Something bigger waiting for me. Little did I know, my dreams were already beginning to take root.

My family was everything to me. We weren't a typical showbiz family. There were no connections, no fame legacy, and no family in Hollywood. I live in a small American town with just my two siblings, a couple of parents, and myself. My dad had a regular office job, and my mom was a stay-at-home mom. Despite their unglamorous careers, they had a work ethic that, as I would come to understand, influenced me more than I could have realized at the time. Surrounded by hardworking neighbors who treasured family time, we lived in a modest home. Nevertheless, they encouraged me to pursue my dream even though it appeared unattainable.

The moment it all changed seems like it happened yesterday. One afternoon, while I was playing with my dolls in the living room, my mother approached me and handed me a brochure from a nearby talent agency. We didn't talk about it very often. Our family wasn't particularly interested in acting as a career. However, there was a tiny spark—a possible chance. My mother suggested that I try it after noticing the joy in my eyes whenever I would discuss the TV actors or mimic their voices.

I wasn't entirely sure what it would mean at the time. I had no idea how drastically my life would change or how much work it would require. It just sounded like fun to me. Attending auditions and appearing in commercials seemed like such an exciting and promising prospect. My mother drove me to my first audition, I recall. Trying to picture myself in front of a camera and trying to look as poised and "cool" as the actresses I saw on TV made me anxious but also excited. I quickly came to the conclusion that this was not all fun and games. Rejection was inevitable, and auditions were stressful. Not every role was given to me, and occasionally none at all. That didn't stop me, though. It stoked my fire, if anything.

Learning the ropes was the main focus at first. A strange but fascinating world was presented to me. My first genuine look at the industry was during the auditions. As anxious as I could be, I would enter those casting rooms and observe the other children, wondering if they shared my feelings of excitement, fear, hope, and doubt. I soon discovered that being "good" wasn't the only thing that went into acting; it was also about being unique, getting attention, and possessing something that others didn't. I could feel the pressure to perform well and be the best version of myself in front of total strangers, even though I wasn't yet aware of how complicated what I was doing was.

The callbacks followed.

It was unlike anything else. It felt significant to be invited back for a second round of auditions. It seemed like a minor triumph. But I also began to see that this world wasn't always kind or fair. There were ten more unsuccessful auditions for every callback. And ten more roles slipped through my fingers for every one I nearly got. But as a kid, I persevered because of the thrill and optimism of every new chance. Even though I was aware that my chances were slim, I felt that I had something unique to contribute and that I was destined to be there.

I had to constantly strike a careful balance between being a child and following my dreams during these formative years. The world beyond your family and friends can seem vast and overwhelming to a child. For me, acting was about preserving my childhood, not just about learning lines and attending auditions. Even though I felt pressure to mature rapidly, I still needed the simple pleasures of youth, like playing outside with friends and discussing my school day with my parents over dinner. My family made every effort to ensure that I didn't forget that. They ensured that I attended school, completed my assignments, and had time to be a child.

It was challenging to keep that balance at times. My personal life was beginning to suffer from the demands of the acting industry. Weekends were spent at auditions instead of with friends, and school assignments became scripts to memorize. The young child who merely desired to dress up began to feel the burden of her own aspirations. However, my family, especially my mother, reminded me to maintain my groundedness. She would frequently advise me to have big dreams but to keep in mind that life is more than just your on-screen persona. It was about spending time with the people you cared about.

Getting my first real role was one of my favorite memories from those early days. Even though it was only a little commercial, it felt significant. It gave me my first taste of what it was like to work with a crew, be on a set, and have my performance realize someone else's vision. I had never felt anything like the excitement of being in front of the camera. Everything felt so significant—the crew, the lights, the script. The feeling of finally being acknowledged for something I had worked so hard to achieve, however, is what I remember most. One could feel the excitement. I became enamored.

I started receiving more auditions over time. Some were advertisements, some were small TV show roles, and some were just me trying to get a job. It wasn't simple. There were nights when I would lie awake wondering if this dream would ever come true, and days when I felt like I was making no progress. However, I was also motivated by a strong sense of pride. My resolve was strengthened by my parents' pride in me. I wanted to show them and myself that I was capable of doing this.

I persisted in spite of the obstacles, the auditions, the rejections, and the protracted waits. I clung to the belief that the right role would eventually present itself and that I would be prepared.

Everything that followed was built upon those formative years. I learned patience, humility, and perseverance from them. They taught me that although dreams don't materialize right away, you get closer to your goals with each step, audition, and minor triumph. I also had a sneaking suspicion that the journey was far from over.

Chapter 2

The Road Less Traveled

"The road to success is always under construction."

I had no idea this quote would be so accurate when I first began my acting career. It took effort, perseverance, and continuous dream reconstruction rather than merely skill or good fortune. It frequently seemed like there were two steps back for every step forward. However, the effort was worthwhile. In retrospect, I see that those times of uncertainty, annoyance, and rejection were all necessary steps in the process. They helped mold me into the actor and person I am today.

My career didn't start off with a lot of success right away. Not at all. I still recall how anxious and excited I was when I first started going to auditions. Because of the enthusiasm I brought to those auditions, my passion for acting, and my unwavering will to succeed, I believed I would get a role soon. But soon, reality set in. The rejections came quickly and frequently. At first, I couldn't figure out why I wasn't getting the parts for which I tried out. Why was I stuck with "thank you, but we've decided to go in a different direction" emails while other kids were getting callbacks and parts?

Those rejections hurt at first. Refusing to take them personally was difficult. I started to doubt myself because every "no" felt like a kick to the stomach. Was I inadequate? Was I not gifted enough? Is there anything else I should be doing with my life? Trying to blend in with my peers while juggling the demands of my acting ambitions made school difficult enough. In addition to all of that, I felt like I was failing.

It was never easy to balance auditions and school. On certain days, I would come home from school early in order to prepare for an audition. I would put on a front, make an effort to appear assured, and enter that casting office with the hope that I would be selected today. The energy required to sustain that level of focus, particularly as a teenager attempting to mature and navigate life at the same time, is something that is frequently overlooked. The difficulties of school included friendships, homework, and all the other things that come with being a young person. I was also under pressure to manage a part-time job while I was a student, keep up with the business side of acting, and audition for roles that I might or might not get.

I sometimes thought I was living two lives: one as a typical adolescent and another as a budding actress attempting to make a name for myself. My mind would be racing about my audition earlier that morning as I sat in a classroom trying to concentrate on my studies. I recall feeling the pressure of juggling homework and learning lines for the next role after racing out of school in the hopes of making it to my audition. I would attempt to enjoy the routine of being just another high school student on the few days when I didn't have auditions, but I was still unable to avoid the pressure of what was ahead. At times, I wasn't sure how to handle everything.

These feelings of uncertainty persisted for a while. Even after a few successful auditions, they stayed for a while. I asked myself over and over again: Was this worth it? Would I ever succeed? The doubt hovered over me like a shadow, never going away. To be honest, I had no idea what the answers were at the time. All I knew was that I couldn't give up. I had to continue.

I made an effort to take comfort in the little triumphs during those formative years. I would get a bit role on a TV show or a small part in a commercial. They were stepping stones, but they weren't the significant breaks I had hoped for. Every time I walked onto a set, I gained new knowledge, and every "yes" made the "no's" easier to accept. I made an effort to put my all into every role, no matter how small. I wanted to make every moment matter; I wasn't content to just get by. Every encounter, no matter how minor, helped me grow.

Even though I made an effort to maintain my optimism, there were still days when I felt like I was not making any progress. Sometimes I would sit by myself in my room and look up at the ceiling, wondering if I should give up. Would my dreams be merely that—dreams—forever? Everyone seemed to be moving more quickly than I was, and the acting industry felt very competitive. It was discouraging to see other kids get bigger roles, book series, and recognition while I had trouble finding steady employment. The fear of falling behind was more important than success or notoriety.

But as time passed, I came to understand something crucial: the destination wasn't the point. The journey was the main focus. I had to have faith that my efforts would eventually be rewarded and that the right role would present itself. I therefore persisted in moving forward, step by step, through one audition after another, and even through one rejection after another.

Then it happened one day. I received the call that would alter my life. When I was informed that I had advanced to the final round for a role that felt different, I had been auditioning for years without taking a significant break. It was a project that seemed like it might be my big break, not just another audition. I was trying out for the role of Samantha LaRusso, Daniel LaRusso's daughter, in the film Cobra Kai, which was a reimagining of the popular Karate Kid franchise.

It would be an understatement to say that I was thrilled. Being able to participate in that world was an absolute dream come true for me, as I had grown up watching The

Karate Kid movies. However, I was also aware that this might mark a significant shift in my professional trajectory. There was pressure. Delivering was my responsibility, and I had to do it well. This position was more than just another one; it was the one that could lead to all of the things I had fought for.

I was nervous about the callback, but as soon as I entered the room, something clicked. I saw it as a chance to demonstrate to the casting directors my true self as an actress, not just another audition. I had the opportunity to make Samantha LaRusso come to life in a way that no one else could, and I was no longer just a girl reading lines. I was aware that this was my chance.

I was overcome with emotion when I eventually learned that I had been chosen to play Samantha. It was the result of years of arduous effort, sacrifice, and tenacity; it wasn't just about landing a part. This was the result of all the late nights spent studying lines, all the rejections, and all the moments of uncertainty. But it was a bittersweet sense of victory. Yes, it was a victory, but I was aware that this was just the start of a completely different adventure.

Although getting that role was a significant step, it was only the beginning of a new chapter in the journey. I would encounter fresh obstacles, hardships, and chances for development. However, the discovery demonstrated that the journey, despite its challenges, was worthwhile. It served as a reminder that having a smooth path isn't what defines success; rather, it's about having the fortitude to continue moving forward even when the road is being built.

Knowing that every obstacle I had overcome and every action I had taken had brought me to this point, I continued. I was prepared for whatever lay ahead, even though the journey was still lengthy.

Chapter 3

The Rise of a Fighter

"It's not the challenge that defines you; it's how you rise to meet it."

In life, you can't avoid the challenges that come your way, but you can control how you face them. That's a lesson I've learned time and time again, especially when I think about my journey with Cobra Kai. Landing the role of Samantha LaRusso wasn't just about auditioning for a part—it was about stepping into a legacy, a role that was part of a beloved franchise with fans who had strong connections to the original Karate Kid films. For me, it was the ultimate challenge. But looking back, it was also the moment that made me realize that I had to embrace it, face it head-on, and rise to meet the expectations set before me.

When I first heard about Cobra Kai, I didn't think much of it. Like many people, I assumed it was another reboot or remake of a classic film—one that wouldn't live up to the original. But when I was told that I was being considered for the role of Samantha LaRusso, the daughter of Daniel LaRusso from The Karate Kid, my heart stopped for a second. I was a huge fan of the original films, and the idea of being a part of that universe—of playing a character that was the daughter of a cinematic icon—was beyond exciting. But it also came with a lot of pressure. Samantha wasn't just any character; she was the continuation of a story that had shaped so many people's lives.

I had always admired the Karate Kid films for their themes of resilience, growth, and the struggle between good and evil. The original movie introduced a character in Daniel LaRusso who was relatable—he wasn't perfect, he made mistakes, but he fought for what he believed in. I grew up watching The Karate Kid, like most kids my age, and the idea of being a part of that world felt like a dream come true. But now, with the opportunity to portray his daughter, I had to rise to meet a legacy that was so much bigger than me.

The audition process for Cobra Kai was unlike anything I had ever experienced. It wasn't just about reading lines from a script—it was about bringing something new to a character that had to feel authentic to the original while also being her own person. I spent hours preparing for that first audition. I rewatched The Karate Kid, taking notes on how Daniel's character was portrayed and the nuances of his relationship with his mentor, Mr. Miyagi. I knew that Samantha had to carry the spirit of her father but also be a modern-day version of a young woman struggling to find her identity. The balance between honoring the past and creating something new was something I had to get right.

When I walked into that audition room, I was a bundle of nerves and excitement. I had done my research, I had prepared the best I could, but I knew that in this industry, anything could happen. I looked around at the other actors in the room, all vying for the same role, and I felt both inspired and intimidated. I took a deep breath and reminded myself that I belonged there. This wasn't just another audition for me—it was the chance to show them who I was as an actress and to prove I could take on this challenge.

I read my lines with everything I had, embodying Samantha in that moment. I could feel the pressure, but I also felt something else: a deep connection to the character. She wasn't just a daughter in a movie—she was someone with her own struggles, her own desires, her own battles to fight. As the audition wrapped up, I left the room knowing that I had done my best. The nerves didn't go away, but I felt like I had finally stepped into a role that challenged me in ways I hadn't expected.

Days passed, and the uncertainty of waiting was unbearable. I kept replaying the audition in my mind, wondering if I had done enough. Then, one afternoon, I got the call. I had been cast as Samantha LaRusso. I remember the exact moment I heard the news. It was one of those rare moments when everything in your life seems to stop. I was overwhelmed with excitement and disbelief. This was it—the role that could change everything. But with that excitement also came a flood of responsibility. This wasn't just a job; it was a legacy. And I was going to be part of it.

Stepping into the Cobra Kai world wasn't easy. The first time I walked on set, I was both starstruck and terrified. I was surrounded by talented actors who had been a part of the original Karate Kid series, as well as newcomers who were bringing their own energy to the show. I felt a deep sense of gratitude, but also a sense of intimidation. I had to prove myself. I had to show that I was worthy of stepping into this iconic universe and taking on a role that meant so much to so many people.

The character of Samantha LaRusso was a challenge in itself. On the surface, she was the daughter of a hero, someone who had grown up with a father who was always teaching her about resilience, discipline, and standing up for what was right. But Samantha wasn't a perfect character. She had her flaws, her own struggles with identity, and her own personal battles to face. She was caught between the worlds of her father's legacy and her own desires for independence. She wasn't always the "good girl," and that made her real. She was complex, and portraying her required me to dig deep into my own understanding of what it meant to be both strong and vulnerable.

Samantha's journey in Cobra Kai was one of self-discovery. She wasn't just learning how to fight physically; she was learning how to fight for herself. She struggled with relationships, with her sense of identity, and with finding a place in a world that was constantly changing. What I loved most about playing Samantha was that she was unapologetically human. She wasn't defined by one thing, and her growth mirrored my own growth as an actress. There were times on set when I had to confront my own insecurities, just as Samantha had to confront hers.

The most powerful lesson I took from portraying Samantha was the importance of resilience, both on and off the screen. The show's themes of fighting for what's right, of standing up even when the odds are against you, resonated deeply with me. In a way, playing Samantha forced me to rise to meet the challenges in my own life. Acting is a form of vulnerability—it requires you to put parts of yourself on the line, to face fears and doubts, and to push through them. And just like Samantha, I had to find my own strength in the face of adversity.

The more I worked on the show, the more I realized that Cobra Kai wasn't just about karate—it was about life. It was about embracing the fight, not only with external forces but with ourselves. As an actress, I had to tap into that spirit, to embody someone who was constantly evolving, learning, and fighting for herself. Samantha wasn't just a character on a screen; she was a reminder that the fight we face in life is often the one that defines us.

By the end of the first season, I had not only learned so much about acting but also about life. The challenges I faced in portraying Samantha LaRusso were the same kinds of challenges I faced as a person. I learned to embrace them, to rise to meet them, and to push forward, even when things felt impossible. And in the process, I found a fighter inside of me that I didn't know existed.

The journey was far from easy, but it was worth it. Cobra Kai changed my life in ways I never expected, and the lessons

I learned while playing Samantha will stay with me forever. It wasn't just the role of a lifetime—it was the opportunity to prove that no matter how difficult the road is, the rise is always worth it.

Chapter 4

A New Kind of Hero

"Heroes aren't made in the spotlight; they're made in the shadows."

Heroism, in my opinion, comes from the hardships, the errors, and the development that take place behind the scenes rather than from the flawless, glamorous moments that everyone witnesses. Throughout my time playing Samantha LaRusso on Cobra Kai, this quote has remained with me. Samantha wasn't like other heroes. She didn't always do the "right" thing, and she wasn't always the center of attention. But as the seasons changed, she became someone who taught me that true heroism is found in the flaws—the moments of uncertainty, the difficulties, and the choices to stand up for what's right even when it's difficult.

Samantha was first presented as a young woman torn between her own identity and her father's legacy when I first began playing her. She was attempting to discover her identity in a society that was always expecting her to conform to a certain stereotype, whether it was that of the ideal high school student or daughter. Samantha was initially under a lot of external pressure, including her rivalry with Tory, her father's expectations, and the complex relationships she had with her friends. She wasn't a conventional "hero" in the sense that she was perfect or knew all the answers. Like all of us in our own lives, she was still learning.

I began to notice more facets in Samantha as we progressed through the first few seasons. She was more than just the rule-abiding good girl who aspired to be liked. She was battling with her sense of value and attempting to define herself outside of the chaos of high school drama and her father's shadow. Samantha was still, in a sense, discovering what it meant to be a hero—not by defeating the villains, but by overcoming her own inner struggles. And I could relate to that on a deep level.

I noticed that I was accepting Samantha's complexity more and more as the seasons went on. One aspect of herself did not define her. Her father's teachings had taught her to be calm and disciplined, but she also carried a fire inside of her that came from feeling misunderstood and angry at the world. Without sacrificing Samantha's core identity, I had to figure out how to bring that out. Although she wasn't a villain, she was a teenager going through real feelings and challenges. She made mistakes and was in error at times, and as an actress, I had to let that vulnerability show.

Season 2 was one of the most significant times for Samantha and for me as an actress. Samantha had to face her own privilege, her own fears, and her tense relationship with her father after everything that transpired with Tory and the drama surrounding the school fight. During this season, she truly began to blossom and made the deliberate choice to stand up for herself. You could see that change even though she was still learning how to be a hero in her own right. She was fighting for something that was important to her, not just following the rules. She began advocating for herself, her future, and her identity, not just for her father or those around her.

I find a scene in Season 2 where Samantha and her father, Daniel, have a heated discussion to be particularly memorable. She's finally letting him know that she can't just live up to his expectations of her and that she needs to find her own path. There were a lot of emotions going on at the time, making it difficult to film. In that scene, I recall having a strong emotional bond with Samantha. Finding my own voice in a society that occasionally encourages us to blend in rather than stand out was more important than the character itself.

Samantha's development also forced me to face my own development as an actress. I initially just played the part, but as time passed, I came to see how important it was for me to comprehend Samantha's difficulties in order to give the character realism. Sometimes it was difficult to give her the appropriate amount of emotional depth. I occasionally had to push myself beyond my comfort zone and explore uncomfortable or strange emotions. Being able to distance oneself from the character while still feeling the impact of their experiences is something that I believe many actors struggle with.

However, it was also about Samantha's physical development in addition to her emotional complexity. As the seasons progressed, Samantha started karate training, which I had never done before. I needed to learn how to move, how to fight, and how to be strong and disciplined like Samantha's father would have taught her. Being confident and controlling every move, stance, and punch was more important than simply projecting a tough exterior. To ensure that I could authentically depict Samantha's transformation, I worked with the stunt coordinators for numerous hours. It was very rewarding, but it was also very draining. I also used the physicality of karate to help Samantha develop her growing resilience and strength.

Observing the fans' reactions to Samantha's journey was one of the most fulfilling parts of playing her. I had no idea what to anticipate when Cobra Kai debuted on Netflix. Fans from the first Karate Kid movies were already there, but they belonged to a different generation. Additionally, I noticed how much people related to Samantha as the show gained popularity. They could relate to her because they witnessed her hardships, triumphs, and imperfections. Fans who had grown up watching The Karate Kid were not the only ones who reached out to me; a new generation of viewers was also learning the value of forgiving others, being resilient, and standing up for what's right, like Samantha.

I recall getting messages from admirers who had faced their own challenges, such as bullying, family issues, or figuring out their own identity, and they expressed to me how much Samantha's story had motivated them. Some of them even claimed to have looked up to her as a role model, someone who demonstrated to them that it was acceptable to struggle and be flawed, but also to get back up and keep going. For me, knowing that Samantha's development on screen had an effect in real life was the ultimate reward.

I became more and more aware of how unique this show was as I collaborated with the cast. Our characters' on-screen interactions were a direct result of the relationships we developed off-screen. It was much simpler to give our characters life because of the cast's genuine chemistry. Everyone became close to me, but Mary Mouser, who plays Robby, became more than just a co-star; she became a close friend. We would practice for hours on end, discussing the adventures of our characters and exchanging ideas. I was struck by the electric sense of camaraderie on set and realized how crucial the relationships between the actors are to producing a realistic result.

I am proud of Samantha's journey from the beginning of Cobra Kai to her current position. She began as a young girl attempting to define herself while juggling her own desires with the shadows of her father's legacy. But as time went on, she developed into a fighter in her own right, not just a daughter. And I feel as though I've traveled the same path as her in many respects. In the same way that she overcame her obstacles, I also learned how to confront obstacles head-on as a person and as an actress.

Samantha has taught me that heroes aren't always flawless. They are characterized by how they overcome obstacles rather than by their successes or failures. And while Samantha keeps developing on-screen, I am aware that I am also developing with her, becoming more resilient, stronger, and genuine every day.

Chapter 5

Crafting Her Identity

"Your identity is not defined by your success; it's defined by your journey."

I've been on a journey for as long as I can remember, but I didn't fully comprehend it until I began to think about it. When I first started acting, I believed that getting roles and recognition was the main goal. However, I quickly came to the realization that the person I was growing into along the way was more important than my success or notoriety. In front of and behind the camera, it was about discovering who I was. With time, I realized that my identity would be defined by the decisions I made, the lessons I learned, and the authenticity I brought to everything I did, not by the parts I played or the praise I got.

In many respects, Hollywood can seem like an extreme environment. The glitz and glamour of the red carpets, the premieres, and the celebrity are on the one hand. On the other hand, there are the difficulties and demands that come with being well-known. It didn't take me long to realize how much pressure I was under, both from other people and from within. I didn't want to be a "character actress" or someone who followed a certain mold. I wanted to be recognized as someone who could play a variety of roles, push the envelope, and maintain her composure throughout. But how can you accomplish that when everything around you is changing all the time?

It wasn't always easy to strike a balance between being true to myself and meeting social expectations. There are a lot of comparisons and judgments in the acting industry. It's simple to become preoccupied with what other people are doing, their level of success, or their number of followers. For a long time, I let those external markers define my worth. I believed that I had to continuously prove myself if I wanted to be taken seriously in this field. I had to be the ideal actress, always performing at the highest level and never displaying any signs of weakness. However, the more I pursued that version of myself, the more I forgot what was most important: my genuineness.

I eventually came to see that I could succeed without compromising who I was. And honoring myself and my craft came before pleasing everyone else. I developed the ability to turn down positions that would have kept me in a box and didn't feel like a good fit for me. I began looking for roles that pushed me to grow as an actress and that tested my abilities. I was able to showcase my range as an actress during this time by taking on roles that were entirely different from Samantha LaRusso's character, Cobra Kai.

My most significant project outside of Cobra Kai was a dramatic movie that called for me to use an entirely different range of emotions. In contrast to Samantha, the character I portrayed in that movie was nuanced, unvarnished, and broken. I learned a lot from the experience, including how much I still needed to learn about myself and acting. It wasn't easy because I had to delve deeply into feelings like grief, pain, and vulnerability that I had never examined before. I recall feeling more vulnerable than I had anticipated. However, I gained more self-confidence as a person and as an actress as a result of that experience. It served as a reminder that comfort isn't always the path to growth. It sometimes results from taking risks and being prepared to fail.

I also learned a valuable lesson about the art of acting from that role: it's not about changing who you are; rather, it's about bringing out aspects of yourself that you were unaware of. I learned new aspects of myself—my empathy, my understanding of pain, and my strength in vulnerable situations—by portraying characters that felt so different from who I am. I discovered that in addition to learning how to portray various characters, I was also learning about the depth of human connection, the complexity of human emotions, and the persuasiveness of storytelling.

I never lost sight of Samantha LaRusso, though, and the influence that role had on me. As an actress, Samantha has always played a significant role in who I am. However, playing her also gave me a priceless lesson in resiliency. Samantha was a fighter in her own right, not just a fictional character with physical fighting prowess. She stood up for herself, her beliefs, and the people she cared about. In a sense, I came to see that I was fighting for the roles that would help me develop, for the freedom to express myself, and for the opportunity to remain loyal to my own path.

Throughout Cobra Kai, I witnessed Samantha's and my own evolutionary progress. She started out as a character who had trouble expressing herself. However, she grew stronger, more confident, and more determined to forge her own path as the series went on. Samantha's development paralleled mine in many respects. I was also learning how to maintain my groundedness while juggling the demands of the industry. I was discovering who I was outside of the parts I played and outside of what other people thought of me.

I came to see that accepting the journey was crucial. Growth is not linear and takes time to occur. There were moments when I thought I was failing, when I wasn't sure where I was going or where I fit in the industry. However, those periods of uncertainty were a necessary part of the process. They contributed to the development of both my personal and acting identities. I discovered that it was acceptable to not know everything. It was acceptable to show my vulnerability and to acknowledge when I needed assistance or didn't know something. I discovered more about myself and was better able to inhabit the roles I played the more I accepted that vulnerability.

The importance of remaining true to who I am, however, was perhaps the most significant lesson I took away from my journey. I became more confident in my decisions the more I worked on creating my own identity in both my personal and professional life. Other than myself, I didn't need to prove myself. I didn't have to pursue the same level of success that other people were. I had to do what I felt was right. And I found peace in doing so.

The noise level in Hollywood is high. People are always telling you what to do, who you should be, and how to behave. However, everything changed when I at last understood that those outside factors did not define who I was. I discovered how to follow my gut, be picky about the roles I played, and never accept anything less than what felt real. The goal of this journey was to become a better version of myself, not just a better actress.

I keep these lessons in mind as I develop and advance in my work. My roles now serve to express aspects of who I've come to know along the way, rather than merely impressing people or demonstrating my value. And as I look to the future, I can't wait to keep developing both on and off screen, learning new things, and creating my identity.

Chapter 6

Behind the Camera

"The best films are the ones where everyone brings their own vision to the table."

Being a part of a living, breathing puzzle is somewhat like being on set. Every component, including the director, actors, crew, and writers, is essential to making a story come to life. It's simple for an actress to believe that the magic of filmmaking only occurs in front of the camera. In actuality, however, the true magic takes place in the background. It lies in the cooperation, discussions, adaptations, and common goal that all parties contribute. I had no idea how much I would learn about the craft of filmmaking just by participating in that collaborative process when I first started working in Hollywood.

I was anxious and thrilled when I walked onto a Cobra Kai set for the first time. Nothing could have prepared me for the enormity of it all, even though I had already spent years practicing my lines, going to auditions, and picturing what it would be like to work on a real set. Lighting, sound, costumes, hair, makeup, and cameras were just a few of the numerous moving components. Then there were the connections among the entire crew, the director, and the actors. Telling the best story possible was what everyone was aiming for. However, I soon saw that this objective necessitated a high degree of cooperation and trust.

One of the most crucial elements of my growth as an actress was collaborating with the director. One of Cobra Kai's creators, Jon Hurwitz, sat me down in front of one of my first major scenes early on and told me about his idea for Samantha. In addition to giving me instructions, he inquired about my thoughts on the character, her motivations, and how I perceived her development over the course of the narrative. It was a discussion that gave me the impression that I was actively participating in the process rather than merely acting out lines. The difference was entirely due to Jon's skill at making me feel as though my opinions were valued. It allowed me to fully develop the character and give her my own unique style while still adhering to the show's overarching concept.

However, the director wasn't the only one who collaborated. My performance was greatly influenced by the cast members' chemistry as well. Cobra Kai isn't just about one character; it's also about the dynamics and relationships between the characters. It was an education in and of itself to work with the amazing cast of Cobra Kai, particularly Mary Mouser, Tanner Buchanan, and Billy Zabka. Seeing them bring their characters to life taught me a lot. Being in the present, responding to your surroundings, and paying attention to your scene partner were all more important than simply reciting lines.

Working with individuals who share your enthusiasm for your craft has a profoundly positive impact. Everything fell into place because of the genuine connection we had in a scene where Samantha and Robby (Tanner Buchanan) share an emotional moment. In that moment, a silent understanding was sufficient; no words were required. That is the magic of teamwork. Nothing needs to be forced; it just occurs when you have faith in your co-stars and let them contribute their own interpretation of the plot.

Of course, things weren't always easy. Being a member of a large ensemble cast presented many difficulties. On some days, the energy was low, we worked long hours on set, and the pressure to do everything perfectly seemed unbearable. However, it was during those times that I realized how important teamwork is. We had to rely on one another during times of fatigue in order to maintain concentration, maintain the enthusiasm, and support one another during difficult situations. Just as significant as the on-screen chemistry was the camaraderie that took place behind the scenes.

I remember one scene from Season 2 in particular. Even though I admired Samantha's character's physicality, I was conscious of how physically taxing these scenes were because we were filming a significant fight scene. I had to practice the choreography with the stunt coordinators, and there were times when I was afraid I wouldn't do it correctly. I recall watching Mary Mouser, who portrayed Sam's best friend, enter a fight scene with such ease and assurance. I was inspired by the realization that we were all in this together, not because I was attempting to outdo her. We were all encouraging one another to perform better, take chances, and give it our all.

And I learned important lessons from more than just the actors. My growth was greatly influenced by the crew, particularly the camera operators and cinematographers. As an actor, I had never considered how lighting could drastically alter a scene's mood or how a single camera angle could produce a completely different atmosphere, but these concepts became very significant to me. I started to see how each department and individual on set played a crucial part in determining the finished product. For instance, the director of photography would frequently highlight how specific lighting could improve a scene's mood, and I would modify my performance accordingly. It served as the ideal reminder that making a movie requires collaboration and that no one person can produce a work of art by themselves.

I would occasionally be in awe of the work that was being done all around me. I recall observing the costume designers at work as they created ensembles that told a story in addition to fitting the character's personality. Seeing how even the smallest detail could alter how a character was viewed, I would watch the makeup artists change the actors into completely different people. I was particularly interested in the sound department, which created the ideal atmosphere for every scene. Being around such talented people inspired me to set higher standards for myself, to appreciate the art of filmmaking in general as well as my acting, because they were all so committed to their craft.

The goal of filming Cobra Kai was to become a part of something much greater than simply playing a character. I was learning from people around me every day. My understanding of the subtleties of filmmaking—the perseverance, accuracy, and unwavering dedication to the craft—grew as I watched more. We created something amazing because every individual on the set contributed something special.

As I reflect on my time spent working behind the scenes, I am immensely appreciative of the opportunity. I thought I understood what it meant to be an actress when I first entered the field, but I soon discovered that there was a lot more to it than that. It's about working together. It all comes down to learning, listening, and keeping an open mind. Working with such gifted individuals has allowed me to develop not only as an actress but also as a person. Filmmaking is a delicate dance of creativity.

Ultimately, the real benefit lay in the intimate moments—those brief, behind-the-scenes times when we all joined forces to produce something unique. The core of the story is found in those moments, which have a magic that cannot be repeated. One of the most rewarding parts of my journey was being a part of that process, adding my piece to the puzzle.

Chapter 7

The Power of Social Media

"The power of social media lies in its ability to bridge gaps and build communities."

Social media seemed like an afterthought when I first started working in Hollywood. Even though everyone had a profile and it seemed like a fun way to meet new people, it wasn't until I started getting more involved in the industry that I realized how powerful it was. In those days, social media was just another way to advertise yourself, give your followers a shout-out, or post a behind-the-scenes photo. But as time went on, I came to see how much more it could be—a forum for communication, a place to create communities, and a chance to raise awareness of important issues.

I was abruptly thrown into a far wider public arena when Cobra Kai started to gain popularity and the fan base grew. Fans were engaging with the characters, the stories, and the people who brought them to life in addition to simply watching the show. I quickly started to sense the strength of that connection. People were curious about me as a person, not just as Samantha LaRusso. They were interested in my journey, my thoughts, and my experiences.

I was a little overwhelmed at first. Seeing the excitement and attention was thrilling, but it was also a little frightening. How do you maintain your privacy while disclosing enough about yourself to establish a relationship? How do you manage the demands of the spotlight without sacrificing your authenticity? I found it difficult to accept social media as a means of fostering human connections for a while. I was hesitant to share parts of my life with millions of people because I wasn't used to being that transparent.

However, as I started interacting with my followers, I became aware of how much social media could influence both my professional and personal development. Real people who related to my work and shared their experiences with me were more important than likes or followers. At that point, I began to see social media for what it really is: a means of establishing deep connections. I started posting about the things that were important to me, answering comments, and sharing my opinions about the show. I gradually became more at ease being who I am in this environment.

The ability for fans to participate in the conversation is one of my favorite features of social media. They are active participants rather than merely passive viewers. Fans began messaging me to express how much Cobra Kai had changed their lives, how Samantha's hardships spoke to them, and how the show's lessons had taught them to stand up for themselves. Hearing that my portrayal of Samantha had such an impact on people was humbling, especially since I was still figuring out who I was as a person and as an actress. However, what really stood out to me was how these exchanges helped me connect with people from different backgrounds. I used social media to be a part of something greater than myself, not just to advertise my work.

The time I shared a post about mental health awareness is one instance that comes to mind. Recently, I had been thinking back on my personal experiences with stress and anxiety, particularly during the demanding Cobra Kai filming. I made the decision to talk about it and urge my followers to look after their mental health. The reaction was tremendous. Fans thanked me for being honest about my own mental health issues in the hundreds of messages I received from them. It was one of those times when I became acutely aware of my potential impact—not only as an actress, but also as someone who could encourage others to take better care of themselves and normalize uncomfortable discussions.

I have also advocated for gender equality in the entertainment industry using my platform. As a woman working in Hollywood, I can attest to the value of standing by women who are vying for the same opportunities as men. The response to my post about the need for more equal representation in front of and behind the camera was amazing. Actresses and fans contacted me to share their personal stories and show support for the cause. Seeing how something as basic as a social media post could start genuine discussions and encourage a feeling of unity among those fighting for change was empowering.

These exchanges helped me realize social media's actual potential. Creating an environment where people can interact, exchange ideas, and support one another is more important than merely promoting oneself. In a sense, it evolved into a kind of community building, which I initially didn't fully understand. It is truly unique to be able to connect with people and change their lives, even if it is only slightly. I also became aware of how much of an influence I could have on my followers' lives, just as they had on mine, as I kept interacting with them.

These connections also brought about some unexpected and joyful moments. I recall receiving a message from a fan who said that Cobra Kai had gotten them through a challenging period in their lives. They talked about how Samantha's example of tenacity and self-worth had aided them in overcoming personal obstacles. It was one of those infrequent times when you come to the realization that your work involves much more than just acting; it involves establishing a genuine, meaningful, and significant connection with others. These were the times when I realized how important it is to be transparent with my followers, sharing not only the good but also the bad.

I also used this as a chance to give back. I began using my position to advocate for causes that I supported, such as environmental sustainability and animal rights. Social media gave me a special opportunity to spread the word about causes that were important to me and to reach people who might not have otherwise heard about them. I recall sharing a post about a charity event I participated in, and the response was incredible. In addition to supporting the cause, fans also took action by spreading the word, volunteering, or making donations. It served as a powerful reminder of the ability of social media to inspire people and change the world.

Naturally, there were also times when social media felt too much to handle. Being in the spotlight all the time comes with a certain amount of pressure, which was occasionally difficult to handle. I would occasionally feel negatively affected by unfavorable remarks or criticism, especially when they seemed unfair. However, I eventually learned to accept the good along with the bad and concentrate on the potential benefits. I came to see that, regardless of my level of influence, it was critical to remain loyal to myself and make positive use of my position.

I'm now more appreciative than ever of the social media community I've created as I develop both personally and as an actress. It's a place where I can be authentic, share my experiences, and establish deeper connections with people, not just a means of self-promotion. My followers have taught me so much, and their experiences and the ways they have helped me along the way continue to inspire me. Social media is powerful not only because of how many followers you have, but also because of the connections you make, the discussions you initiate, and the change you can bring about. And I've come to see that's what makes it so beautiful.

Chapter 8

The Next Chapter

"The future belongs to those who believe in the beauty of their dreams."

I can't help but feel anxious and excited about what lies ahead as I look to the future. I've always held the view that the best is still to come and that the chances we envision are just around the corner, just waiting for us to seize them. However, it's acceptable that the road to those dreams isn't always obvious. Uncertainty and the power to influence it through our deeds, passion, and openness to change are what make the future so beautiful.

For me, the future encompasses more than just the roles and projects I will undertake. It's about the path I'm still on, how I'll develop further as an actress, a person, and someone who aspires to change the world. When I reflect on all of my experiences, I genuinely believe that I have learned more than I ever could have imagined. I'm also eager to push myself, discover new avenues, and venture beyond my comfort zone in ways I never would have imagined as I go forward.

Working on fresh and varied projects is one of the things I'm most looking forward to. Cobra Kai was an amazing experience that will always hold a special place in my heart and has influenced my career. However, as an actress, I am aware that I have a lot more in mind. I'm excited to take on challenging roles that force me to experiment with new characters, genres, and emotions. I've always thought that stories have the ability to bring people together, spark discussions, and let us see the world from different perspectives. I want to keep developing my skills and learning more about various facets of acting, whether it be comedy, drama, or even something more avant-garde.

I'm thrilled about the prospect of working behind the camera in addition to performing. I've been considering directing, producing, or even starting my own projects for a while. I've grown to value the entire filmmaking process the more I've collaborated with gifted directors, writers, and producers. Being a part of the entire process of making a story come to life, from the original idea to the finished product, is immensely satisfying. I also want to investigate the creative process from a different angle as my career develops. I want to contribute my own voice, write stories that people can relate to, and be a part of the new generation of entertainers who are influencing the direction of the industry.

I consider the kind of legacy I want to leave behind, not just in Hollywood but in the wider world, even as I look forward to the professional opportunities that lie ahead. Success, in my opinion, is about more than just what we accomplish for ourselves; it's also about the legacy we leave behind, the influence we have on others, and the change we help bring about. For me, that entails utilizing my position and life experiences to promote causes close to my heart, such as gender equality, mental health, or the environment. I want my legacy to include both the work I did off-screen to change the world and the characters I portrayed.

 Finding a balance between ambition and authenticity and remaining loyal to my values are two of the most important lessons I've learned in my career thus far. It's simple to become engrossed in the chase of success, the next position, or the next project, but I've learned that it's equally important to stand back and consider what matters most. The experiences that have affected me the most aren't those that have brought me praise or recognition; rather, they are the times when I was able to establish a deeper connection with someone, whether it was through a fan conversation or my work with different causes. In order to approach the next stage of my career with the same passion and a sense of purpose, I want to maintain that sense of authenticity.

I see a chance to combine my personal interests with my career goals in the future. In addition to continuing to use my influence to push for constructive change, I want to use my platform to spread awareness of causes that are significant to me. From environmental sustainability to social justice, there are a lot of issues that require attention, and I feel obligated to speak up for those who don't always have a voice. As my career develops, I want to make sure that the work I do serves a purpose greater than myself rather than just my own interests. I want to leave behind a legacy like that.

Along with continuing to learn from my experiences and the people I meet along the way, I also hope to keep developing personally. Despite all of its glitz and glamour, Hollywood is still a place where people can develop. It's a place where people from all walks of life come together to create something bigger than the sum of their individual parts and where new ideas are continuously shared. I want to stay humble throughout it all, welcome change, and be receptive to fresh viewpoints. I will always be influenced by the lessons I have learned about community power, resilience, and standing up for what I believe in. They will help me navigate the upcoming phase of both my life and career.

Even though I have no idea what the future will bring, I'm prepared for whatever it may bring. Every new chapter, in my opinion, is a chance to develop, find new aspects of myself, and make a significant contribution to society. The dream is constantly changing and never stays the same. And I'm eager to see where this journey will lead me as I enter the next stage of my career.

So let's move on to the following chapter. To the parts I still haven't performed, the things I haven't made yet, and the difference I want to make. I'm prepared to welcome the future with an open mind, an inquisitive heart, and a burning desire to never stop dreaming.

Conclusion

"Stars are made, not born."

I can't help but notice how much has changed since I first had the dream of becoming an actress as I sit here thinking back on my journey. At times, when the road ahead was uncertain and the rejections were piling up, it seemed impossible. However, in retrospect, I see that each step, difficulty, and moment of uncertainty was a necessary component of the process. I wasn't genuinely shaped by the easy route that brought me here; rather, it was by the detours, the turns, and the perseverance to keep going.

A single instance of success or recognition has nothing to do with the process of becoming a "star," whether in Hollywood or any other industry. It all comes down to persistent work, adaptability, and the capacity to gain knowledge and develop from every encounter. Success and fulfillment take time to manifest, just like stars do. It is the result of perseverance, diligence, and faith in our own abilities.

I've had the honor of experiencing things throughout my career that I could only have imagined. I've played a character that people connected with, collaborated with amazing actors and creators, and been a part of something that changed people's lives all over the world. I've also discovered that the journey is still going strong. There are always new challenges to overcome, new things to learn, and new things to discover. Growth is wonderful because it never really stops, and neither does the chance to advance, create, and have bigger dreams.

The fact that growth isn't linear is the one thing I've learned. Doubt will always arise, but it is precisely in these times that we must test our fortitude and develop our character. They show us how to get up and keep going even when it seems like there is no clear way forward. I've discovered that it's acceptable to be vulnerable, make mistakes, and lack all the answers. We really start to realize who we are, what we can do, and where we're supposed to go next during those times.

I am excited and full of hope as I look to the future. I feel prepared to take advantage of every opportunity that presents itself because the world is full of possibilities. I'm excited to keep expanding on the groundwork that has already been established, whether it be through new roles, artistic pursuits behind the camera, or advocacy work that I'm passionate about. The path ahead is equally as significant as the one that led me here, and I'm confident that I'll continue to grow, push myself, and work to have a positive influence in everything I do.

I hope my story serves as a reminder to anyone reading this—whether they are a budding actor or just someone trying to figure things out—that your path is entirely your own to design. Never lose sight of your dreams, no matter how unattainable they may seem at the moment. Have faith in yourself and remain dedicated to your personal development. Success is something that is earned, developed, and fostered over time; it is never given to someone. Thus, take your time. Have fun, have faith in the process, and know that you are more capable than you think.

My family, my co-stars, the Cobra Kai crew, and, of course, my fans are all people who have helped me along the way, and for that I am immensely thankful. I will take your support with me into the next phase of my life because it has meant the world to me.

What about the future? I'm prepared. Knowing that every step forward is a part of the bigger picture—the tale of a star in the making—I will welcome whatever comes next. I'm excited to see where the journey will lead me, and it's still ongoing. So let's look forward to the future, the lessons that still need to be learned, the dreams that have yet to come true, and the limitless potential that each of us possesses. There is still the best to come.

www.ingramcontent.com/pod-product-compliance
Ingram Content Group UK Ltd.
Pitfield, Milton Keynes, MK11 3LW, UK
UKHW040914271125
9219UKWH00026B/505